MONUMENTS AND MEMORIALS OF THE GREAT FAMINE

CATHERINE MARSHALL

CONTENTS

*How can men feel themselves honoured
by the humiliation of their fellow beings?*
Mahatma Gandhi

Brian Tolle's *Irish Hunger Memorial* (2002) **[Figure 1]** in Battery Park City, New York, offers several points of entry for the viewer. It can be accessed from the street through a passageway, like the entrance to the ancient Irish passage grave at Newgrange. In the passageway, texts inscribed onto the walls and an aural accompaniment offer facts and commentaries about the Great Famine in Ireland in the 19th century, and the politics of food around the world today. Alternatively spectators can climb straight onto the sloping plot of land and follow a circuitous path through its unyielding ground to the ruined stone cottage in the center. Other loftier views are afforded from the secure heights of the towering offices of New York's financial sector that surround it. Either way, the path is like a great question mark. Why is this site abandoned? Where have the occupants gone? What is it doing here?

Commemorative projects, born out of memories that often are conflicting, are inherently problematic. In the catalog to his exhibition "Naming the Fields," painter Hughie O'Donoghue wrote about the apparent paradox of memory. "Although it [memory] is not always accurate it is always true; it tries to present the truth as it is felt" (6). Faithfulness to historical accuracy offers no guarantee of emotional satisfaction and at the very least, is always compromised by selectivity. Sometimes historic detail, because of the trauma it engenders, defies the act of representation. Yet the burden of human history must be accepted and faced if we are to understand ourselves. Commemorative projects are nuanced and complicated by a multiplicity of issues: the perspectives and motives of those who originate and execute them, whether they are the victors and perpetrators or victims and their descendants, the often partisan and divisive nature of the evidence, the complexity of the original contexts and the often conflicting agendas of recording and commemorating. We must be constantly aware as well, as historian Mary Daly told a conference devoted to the commemoration of the Easter Rising of 1916 that, whatever else it may be, "commemoration is always political."

Figure 1 | Brian Tolle, *The Irish Hunger Memorial*

5

To what degree do Irish attempts to commemorate the Great Hunger of the 19th century bear out Jean François Lyotard's contention that the very specificities of commemorative projects undermine other readings of historic events and deny wider ownership of them? Lyotard argues that the grand narrative tradition of public memorials denies individual experience. That tradition also may prevent representation of certain kinds of experience altogether. The issue here is not merely that of reconstructing the individual and personal in history, but that the concept of "grandness" fits some historic events more than it does others. This difficulty lies at the heart of the representation of Irish and other post-colonial histories, as well as histories of class and gender conflict. Holocaust studies, like studies of the Irish Famine, highlight the great need to both tell a history and to erase it. They help us to understand the consequent impact of such strategies on the psychological state of generations of survivors of trauma and their need for catharsis (if this is ever possible). It is a project at the very heart of cultural identity and well-being.

Discussing the wide range of positions reflected in Irish Famine commemoration and its relation to history, Margaret Kelleher cites the fears of historians and cultural commentators aroused by recent attempts by journalists to offer psychological interpretations of the past.[2] They fear that some journalistic commentary diminishes real historical research and is directed toward less critical audiences as in John Waters's linking of exuberant spending during the Celtic Tiger and subsequent passivity in the face of economic collapse to Famine history (Waters 29).[3] Patsy McGarry's direct connecting of child sex abuse to the changes in Irish society in the aftermath of the Famine is another example of this passivity. The psychological approach however has support from academic quarters too. Terence Brown believes that:

The black-humour of so much of our literature, our moods of desperation, our compulsive, fearful materialism, our pessimistic expectation of failure, our sense of national incompletion, of silence as our truest language, having lost the national tongue, of hunger as the defining appetite, stronger than the desire to procreate, can all be traced to the Famine (13).

Daly called on historian colleagues to widen their perspectives by looking at the folklore of the Famine as a source of information about it (Póirtéir 607).[4] That invitation has been taken up by Cathal Póirtéir who argues that folklore humanizes the statistics on which history depends (604). By restoring the shared stories of the people to the factual data of history, folklore makes the project of commemorating the Great Famine possible.

Concerns have been expressed by David Lloyd and others about the over-simplified conflation of individual experience into the collective of history[5] and the coarsening of history by the construction of commemorative monuments, which are thought to provide opportunities for closure over the events they mark. The French philosopher and Holocaust survivor, Sarah Kofman, argued for the privileging of the historic over the subjective, but insisted that it was right to mix collective history with autobiography, because historians often disagree. Public memorials bring together the collective in the form of the communities hosting/commissioning them, the individual artist who creates them and the individual historic moment they chose to commemorate. By so doing they can, paradoxically, allow us to forget as Lyotard and Irit Rogoff (97–114) argue. They assert that the imposition of a symbolic object in place of an absence, creates a new presence, with the potential for new memories, but does not satisfy the sense of loss caused by the historic event that it displaces.

Holocaust studies, like studies of the Irish Famine, highlight the great need to both tell a history and to erase it

Ultimately, what should be remembered is that the construction of a historic monument is a creative act, and not an act of historic research, however much this might form part of the process. For this reason, it may be more useful to look at the visual forms surrounding the memorializing project as artwork rather than as historic record. These include the critical context out of which the commemorative projects emerge, the tradition of the grand monument, the commissioning circumstances and the relationship of a commemorative project to its physical and cultural surroundings. These factors shape the final projects at least as much as they are nuanced by either history or theoretic discourse. Discussing his New York monument, Tolle summed up the relationship between the artist and the historical source for many artists:

History functions for me like a raw material. The idea of research as it applies to my work is really about a level of engagement... I don't approach history trying to prove a theory... Over time this relationship grows more intense and matures. If I am lucky enough something materializes in the form of a work, yet this is something I can't predict. In other words, I am not trying to assume the role of a historian ("Interview" 2).

Figure 2 | Glenna Goodacre, *Anguish*

Research into Ireland's Great Hunger involves geography as much as it does history. Location has a powerful influence on the commemorative task. The legacy of dispersal, not to mention feelings of worthlessness and humiliation that the events of 1845–52 cast far into the future means that anyone studying Famine memorials must familiarize themselves with those places in Ireland that resonate still with the memories of that time, and with those places to which the Irish migrated: the United States, Canada, Australia, Britain. The importance of this has been raised by Ciaran Benson, who argues that the self is tied to location and that we cannot really know who we are if we are separated from our place and the stories of our past. Benson is not concerned with promoting nationalism, but with the therapeutic aspect of cultivating the relationship between self and location. It was fear of the former that led the British government in 1842 to prematurely end the gathering of information for the Ordnance Survey Memoir, which had been researching historical monuments in Ireland county by county. The *Freeman's Journal* recognized the government's motive: "Rulers feel uneasy when nations destined to serfdom have such recollections—better they should die out. And this desirable consummation is likely to be attained if our governors have only the determination to forbid completion of the work." Understanding the role of history and commemoration in the shaping of identity has a long history in Ireland.

A study of the constructed evidence—the actual monuments to the Great Hunger—can tell us a considerable amount about commemorative projects. Many commentators have pointed to the absence of Famine memorials until recent decades, an absence so great as to suggest cultural amnesia, though lack of money to commission and build memorials was also an important factor. Ireland remained a colonized country until the establishment of the Free State in 1922 and the colonial establishment did not favor monuments to Irish history while many of those that were built in the country prior to that date celebrated British Imperial achievement and were vandalized rather than enjoyed by the increasingly nationalist Irish population. Commemorative sculptures of the 1798 rebellion in Wexford and Enniscorthy by Oliver Sheppard from 1898 onward were recognized as exceptional by Sir Thomas Grattan Esmond in his speech at the laying of the foundation stone for the Wexford monument in November 1898 (Turpin 71). Brigadier V. R. I. Doyle, uncle of the writer Arthur Conan Doyle, was among those who did not think it possible to represent Irish nationalist subjects under colonial rule. As the son of an artist and brother of Richard Doyle, the noted Victorian painter and cartoonist, and of Henry Doyle, director of the National Gallery of Ireland (1869–92), he was clearly well-informed about the conditions governing art production. A sketch found among his papers after his death showed a drawing of a Celtic cross, which he conceived as a memorial for Lord Edward Fitzgerald, the slain leader of the 1798 Rebellion against the British. It is accompanied by a note saying that when Ireland regained her own parliament, the construction of the monument might be one of the first acts of commemoration carried out under the new regime.

However, even when money and the freedom to choose the subject of commemorative projects became available, giving rise to the 1798 monuments, to the granting of Catholic Emancipation, to the Easter Rising and to other moments from history, almost nothing was proffered as a monument to the Great Hunger. In this, Irish culture merely followed in the tradition of public monuments laid down in other countries, which sought to commemorate and inspire heroic action, rather than to mark a trauma that was still too close to living memory, or that primarily affected the poor and ordinary people. Taking his cue from such eminences as Voltaire and the writers of the French Enlightenment, Thomas Davis wrote in the first issue of *The Nation* (October 15, 1842) of remembrance of the heroic past as a source of inspiration for behavior in the present:

When we speak of high art, we mean art used to instruct and ennoble men, to teach them great deeds whether historical, religious or romantic; to awaken their piety, their pride, their justice and their valour [;] to paint the hero, the martyr, the rescuer, the lover, the patriot, the friend, the saint and the saviour.

commentators have pointed to the absence of Famine memorials until recent decades, an absence so great as to suggest cultural amnesia

The story of mass death from the indignity of starvation and disease did not fit that tradition. Margaret Kelleher has drawn attention to an important but pervasive subtext relating to gender in representations of famine in Ireland and India. In describing the many instances of the personification of famine suffering as female, Kelleher's attention is largely directed toward literary expression, but the visual arts provide an interesting extension to her research. Kelleher looks at the dislocation between the representation of famine as a skeletal, suffering woman, with or without dead or starving children, and the facts as ascertained from statistics. She points out that there is little difference in mortality levels between adult men and women during the famines she discusses, and such differences as there are seem to indicate that women survived in greater numbers, while the heaviest losses occurred among children and the elderly. The personification of famine as adult female, therefore, relates not to the actual event but to patriarchal culture, which sees woman as other, as nature, which the creative man turns to art. Most of the written accounts that Kelleher references are by men, and of the public monuments to the Great Hunger in Ireland, the majority are the work of male artists.

Figure 3 | Erskine Nicol, *A Knotty Point*

The trope of the passive, suffering woman is evident, for example, at the Famine memorial at Reilig an tSléibe, near Dungarvan, Co. Waterford, and *An Gorta Mór* memorial on the Lahinch to Ennistymon Road in Co. Clare; and even works by American female artists Glenna Goodacre [Figure 2] and Margaret Lyster Chamberlain at Ireland's Great Hunger Museum at Quinnipiac University continue this theme.

If we look back at representations of the Famine in painting—a form of visual expression more open to female artists historically—we find a more varied picture. As discussed above, very few visual representations of the Famine existed in the 19th century. While a considerable number of paintings by Erskine Nicol exist from the mid-19th century, they generally show well-fed, but lazy and scheming Irish men and women whose children are neglected, while they drink or gamble [Figure 3]. Famine and the harsh accounts of its impact, so prolific in written accounts from the time, very rarely intrude into Nicol's work. It is not hard to explain this. Nicol was Scottish and his work was offered for sale in Britain where it gave comfort to those who perpetuated the idea that the Irish were to blame for their own difficulties and were not deserving of British generosity, not to mention government aid. A much smaller and generally more sympathetic body of paintings by English artists such as George

Frederic Watts, Frederick Goodall, Francis William Topham and Alfred Downing Fripp also survives from this period but they are few in number. Apart from Daniel MacDonald's *Discovery of the Potato Blight in Ireland* (1847, University College Dublin, Folklore Department), Daniel Maclise's passionate attempt to point up the suffering in Ireland in a disguised allegorical form in his monumental painting of *The Marriage of Strongbow and Aoife* (c. 1854, National Gallery of Ireland), Edwin Hayes's *An Emigrant Ship, Dublin Bay, Sunset* (1853, National Gallery of Ireland) and Robert George Kelly's *An Ejectment in Ireland* (1848–51, private collection), there are few paintings by Irish artists, male or female, about this terrible event or its aftermath from the immediate period. Kelly's painting aroused unfavorable notice in the House of Commons in 1852. English artists could depict such subjects without hostile comment, but Irish artists, it seemed, had to be more careful, if they wanted to sell their work.

there are few paintings by Irish artists, male or female, about this terrible event or its aftermath from the immediate period

Female artists, however, most notably, Lady Elizabeth Butler, Margaret Allen and Lilian Lucy Davidson were to the fore in dealing with the hardship of eviction and emigration arising out of the Great Hunger, and in their work the emphasis is subtly altered. In Butler's *Evicted* (1890, University College Dublin), a painting of an eviction that she actually witnessed, the woman is heroic. In another, of young men forced to seek employment in the British army after they have been evicted, there is sympathy, but no condescension. The former attracted the attention of the British Prime Minister, Lord Salisbury, when shown at the Royal Academy in 1890, leading to his fatuous remark that "I long to take part in an eviction myself, either in an active or passive sense"(Usherwood and Spencer-Smith 95). Margaret Allen painted a moving emigration picture, *The Last Hour in the Old Land,* (1876, private collection), and a number of paintings of political subjects, including *Bad News in Troubled Times* (1886, IGHM) a direct reference to the arrest of three Fenian rebels in Manchester (one of whom may have been a relative), while Lilian Lucy Davidson's *Gorta* (IGHM) **[Figure 4]**, previously referred to as *Burying the Child,* represents a whole family, male and female alike, brought low by tragedy. One of the participants in Davidson's picture directly challenges the viewer to engage with the horrific subject.

Following the Cromwellian plantations in the 17th century and the imposition of British rule over the whole island of Ireland, the dispossessed Irish sought solace for their defeats in poems and songs by male poets that personified the country as a beautiful woman (*spéirbhean*), who visited the poet in a dream (*aisling*) and called for his help to liberate her. The tradition continued through the 19th century, famously repeated by James Clarence Mangan in his poem "Dark Rosaleen" (1846), before he himself succumbed to disease and died in a pauper's ward in a Dublin hospital. Irish men felt shamed by their inability to meet that call from Mangan and the *aisling* poets. It is hard now to comprehend their despair when they found themselves unable not only to measure up to their visionary songs, but also to feed their dying children. Arguably, women, ignored in that tradition and less publicly identified as providers and defenders of home and nation, were better able to deal with the tragedy. Perhaps that is why Irish male artists could not begin to face this history until the bubble of prosperity in the late 1990s restored morale and gave them the opportunity, not just to make art about the Famine but to make it, expensively and assertively, in bronze.

Figure 4 | Lilian Lucy Davidson, *Gorta*

Figure 5 | Paul Henry, *Cottages, West of Ireland*

There were other reasons too for avoiding the subject of famine. Seeking signifiers of a visual identity to offset the first signs of international modernism associated with the old Imperial regime, the conservative Irish Free State in the 1920s channeled its scant interest in the visual arts into the promotion of artists like Paul Henry who offered a particular image of Ireland [Figure 5]. Through beautiful but formulaic paintings of the western seaboard, Henry provided an image of an Ireland unaffected by outside influences, one that was primitive but homely, with cozy cottages and turf stacks, lapped by lakes and protected by high mountains. The viewer's ownership of the scene laid out for his/her gaze is rarely challenged by the occupants of the place, who are generally not shown, or if they are, are presented as types in a landscape that is inviting rather than tragic. Famine had depopulated the West and left the countryside strewn with abandoned, crumbling cottages, and though mass poverty persisted, which the Free State did little to relieve, this is rarely evident in Henry's paintings. That this was the result of a deliberate choice by the artist can be inferred from the fact that he had spent the years from 1910 to 1919 living on

Achill Island, where the signs of Famine devastation are still visible everywhere. Instead, the welcoming charm his landscapes projected was quickly taken up as bait for tourists. The London Midland and Scottish Railway Company Steamers published advertisements for trips to Ireland with paintings of Connemara by Henry, one of which proclaimed in 1926 that it "illustrates in a striking manner a typical phase of Irish scenery. Ireland—the new post-war Ireland—is now ready to welcome the English tourist, and wishes you to explore the beauties of her coast and countryside…" (Walker).

the official silence surrounding the Famine remained unbroken until the 1990s

The war, so tactfully referred to here, is not the World War of 1914–18, but rather the War of Independence against Britain.[6] Clearly, British travel agencies and Irish governments alike were now ready to put former animosities aside in the interest of commerce. The British public, wary of visiting Ireland during that period of insurrection, took up the invitation in great numbers. Henry's paintings continued to be used on Irish tourist posters until the 1960s. Removing traces of the Famine was essential to furthering the holiday atmosphere.

Perhaps we should not be surprised then, that when the first centenary of the beginning of the Great Hunger came in 1945/6, the government avoided it completely. With poverty, unemployment and emigration still prevalent around the country, it chose to host an exhibition of painting and sculpture of historical subjects at the National College of Art in Dublin, but shied away from naming the exhibition after the most cataclysmic event in the country's past, preferring instead to title it *The Thomas Davis and Young Ireland Movement Centenary Exhibitions of Pictures of Irish Historical Interest*. Although this exhibition did contain a number of artworks that referenced the Famine, including Davidson's *Gorta*, it was not the primary focus. Other grand narratives willingly undertaken by governmental agencies, the church, local authorities and emigrants' organizations during this period included monuments to Cúchulainn, Wolfe Tone, Robert Emmet, Charles Stewart Parnell, Patrick Pearse, Jim Larkin and various literary, political and religious figures, as well as to the sinking of the *Lusitania* in Cork and various events during the War of Independence and Civil War. Yet, apart from one prominent exception, the official silence surrounding the Famine remained unbroken until the 1990s. What might have been described as amnesia had begun to look like suppression.

The reasons for this were not hard to find. Rampant poverty and disease never accord with the desired official imagery of any country; commercial interests inevitably influence what can be made, sold and paid for; and images of heroic endeavor are generally thought to be more uplifting and better for public morale, at least in the short term. Irish people could not begin to process the psychological impact of the loss of one quarter of its population to hunger, disease and emigration in a concentrated seven-year period. What made it even more difficult was the continuing presence of appalling poverty. Dublin, under the Union, had the worst slums in Europe in 1911, and while health and hygiene conditions improved in the Free State over the next decades, large numbers of people continued to die from tuberculosis, and emigration rates remained high throughout most of the twentieth century. In these circumstances, there was no possibility of any real sense of closure to the trauma of the Famine. Perhaps it is to be expected then, that until the 1980s, few Irish people could even contemplate Famine commemoration in an officially sanctioned context.

Most commemorative projects result from public commissions. Gradually at first, an increasingly confident, more prosperous and better educated Irish public was in a better position to face repressed memories. Some of the earliest indications of this took the form of writing in Irish. Seosamh Mac Grianna's "Ar an Tráigh Fholamh" is a searing account of death by hunger in coastal Donegal. Mac Grianna's collection of short stories *An Grádh agus an Ghruaim*, in which this story was published was required reading for Irish teenagers taking the Leaving Certificate examination from the year of its publication in 1929 until the late 1960s. Following equally powerful writing by Liam O'Flaherty (*Famine*, 1937), Patrick Kavanagh (*The Great Hunger*, 1942) and Tom Murphy (*Famine*, 1977), artworks dealing directly with the Famine began to appear. The earliest of these were local and individual initiatives, such as the 50-foot high lattice cross, erected by William "Jack" Sorensen, a Cork taxi-driver, in the paupers' cemetery at Carr's Hill, Carrigaline, which may have been inspired by the first centenary of the Great Famine. Sorensen made the work himself in his own garden in the 1950s and personally tended it until his death two decades later. Other local initiatives, like Sorensen's, took the form of simple crosses, often Celtic crosses in cemeteries. Emotionally powerful in their anonymity and modesty, they make no claims for artistic status or insightful historical commentary. Edward Delaney's *Famine* (1967) [Figure 6] sculptural group follows a different trajectory. Tucked into the corner of Saint Stephen's Green in Dublin, it articulates the obverse of his nationalist, commemorative statue of Wolfe Tone, from which it is concealed by a screen of standing stones. Delaney was given a state commission for this memorial to Wolfe Tone. Asked why he had surrounded the fountain at its rear with figures of starving and dying people, the artist said that it represented the failure of Tone's attempts to overthrow British rule in Ireland in 1798. *Famine* was possible in 1967 only because it was part of a bigger project to mark Tone's republican activity, a heroic moment in Irish history. Delaney's evident sympathy for the starving figures owed as much

17

to his first-hand experience as a student of post-war poverty in Germany, as it did to Famine memories in Ireland. Inspired also by Alberto Giacometti's post-Holocaust, skeletal figures, Delaney said, "I wanted to make statues ... so that other people might see in bronze these symbols of the mystery of agony—and life surviving in spite of agony" (Arnold). The irony of the positioning of Delaney's memorial, directly across but tactfully hidden from the Shelbourne Hotel, one of the most prominent symbols of wealth and power in the country, and already well-established when the Great Famine struck, would not have been lost on the artist. The sense of helplessness, shame and loss of dignity that accompanies abject poverty, so well evoked in this work, is rendered even more telling in such an environment.

an imaginative way of remembering that focuses on positive emotions of love and paved the way for the climate that encouraged an official British apology for the Irish Famine in 1997

The most persuasive and powerful of the early artistic responses to the Famine was a body of work by a then young artist, Alanna O'Kelly, who presented an articulate, alternative, feminist approach to the subject. A mixture of experiences inspired her works, which took the form of performances, photographic works and tape/slide installations embodying sound and text as well as imagery. Anti-Irish racism fueled by IRA bombing activities in London in the 1980s, her family roots in Connemara, images of famine in the developing world, and her own powerful empathy with parents struggling to feed their children, led O'Kelly to engage with Irish experience, particularly of hunger. The work that emerged over a period of five or six years from the late 1980s to 1994, when she won the Irish Museum of Modern Art (IMMA)/ Glen Dimplex Artist's Award, was not commissioned. Nor was it dictated by any public agenda. Instead, it grew directly out of a sense that the work simply had to be made.

Using a variety of ingredients—from voices singing in the Irish language, records from the workhouses where the destitute went to die, photographs and video clips of landscapes imbued with this history in the form of lazy beds and human bones and images of nature and nurture alongside aural referents to parts of the modern world where famine is still a regular occurrence, O'Kelly created a trilogy of tape/ slide installations (later translated to DVD) and photographic works. One of these,

Figure 7 | Alanna O'Kelly, *No Colouring Can Deepen the Darkness of Truth*

Sanctuary/Wasteland (1994–1998), was later acquired by the IMMA, while another, *No Colouring Can Deepen the Darkness of Truth* (1994–2012) **[Figure 7]**, formed part of the inaugural collection at Ireland's Great Hunger Museum at Quinnipiac University, and is also permanently installed, as the only item, in the restored workhouse in Carrick-on-Shannon, Co. Leitrim. Most significantly O'Kelly learned how to keen, the traditional mourning ritual performed by Irish women over their dead. In *Sanctuary/Wasteland* she keens for the dead and goes on to sing a lament in Irish which, like keening, was almost wiped out as the Famine devastated the strongholds of old Gaelic culture. Recent writings by Paul Ricoeur and others, inspired by Sigmund Freud's distinction between mourning (an active engagement) and melancholy (a disabling state), speak of the importance of mourning, not just as a cathartic process, but also as a process of working through the complex legacy of the past. O'Kelly's work can be described as an imaginative way of remembering that focuses on positive emotions of love and paved the way for the climate that encouraged an official British apology for the Irish Famine in 1997.

In their clear avoidance of a single narrative, a single mode of communication, or a prescriptive way of looking at events, these artworks undermine older perceptions of what a commemorative artwork or a memorial should be. As tape/slide or DVD installations, they require time as well as space; they cannot be comprehended in a single empowering glance, foreclosing the possibility of instant judgment. They are non-didactic, leaving viewers to absorb them and to take responsibility for their own responses. They are located inside modern museums, where they are not likely to be shown permanently. That means that, like the viewer, their appearance is flexible and sporadic, dependent on public demand or curatorial decision. Unlike permanently erected public monuments, which could be said to colonize the spaces they occupy, these video installations await the viewer on equal terms. Where monuments tend to occupy public space and are therefore experienced publicly, the effect of entering an O'Kelly installation is to be alone with the images and sounds in a darkened space. Responses are thus primarily individualized. Yet they are located in museums, suggesting a level of importance that placement in a private collection can rarely offer. Furthermore, their place in museum collections calls attention to them as works of art as well as commemorative projects.

an Ireland that could now, finally, afford (not just financially, but also psychologically) to look at the absence of commemorative memorials

Only one of these artworks is installed on a permanent basis. A second edition of *No Colouring Can Deepen the Darkness of Truth* is installed inside one of the women's dormitories of the Carrick-on-Shannon Workhouse, part of which functions to this day as a care home and part of which has been painstakingly restored as a Famine memorial. Outside, a graveyard holds the remains of many of those who died in that very ward. O'Kelly had no idea when making this work that the building would one day be restored for its present purpose, so it is coincidental that some of the footage used in the work is of pages from the log book of this actual workhouse. In this context, the installation functions in a very different way from when it is shown in a museum alongside other artworks. In the workhouse, it connects immediately with the viewer, not just imaginatively to the Famine, but to the reality of the dismal surrounding and the unmarked burial mounds outside, while the work itself links that past to contemporary famine in the Global South. Unlike more traditional monuments, O'Kelly's installations can be shown in different places and situations. What they bring to each new location is the breadth and scope of the imagery and sound, uniting history and the present, the collective and the individual, raising issues about time and space in each new location and context. While Delaney's memorial aims to remind contemporary audiences of the devastation, these works by O'Kelly encourage a process of grieving, an active engagement with the history, an opportunity to work with what David Lloyd has referred to as Ireland's "unworked-through loss" (215). Above all, they remind us that hunger and famine have not gone away.

The grand tradition of publicly commissioned sculpture is evoked in the commemorative monuments created by John Behan *(National Famine Memorial,* Murrisk, Co. Mayo, 1997 **[Figure 8]**, and *Arrival,* United Nations Plaza, New York, 2000 **[Figure 9]**) and Rowan Gillespie *(Famine,* Custom House Quay, Dublin, 1997, and *The Arrival,* Ireland Park, Toronto, 2007). Made from cast bronze, the material most closely associated with public monuments, and positioned permanently in prominent public locations, the physical monumentality of these works is not in question. Unlike O'Kelly's very personal creative project, they were commissioned— Behan's by the Irish Government and Rowan Gillespie's Dublin monument, privately by businesswoman Norma Smurift, and others. Since bronze or cut stone are the traditional materials for public commemorative monuments, it is almost inevitable that major commissions for commemorative monuments were, until very recently, directed toward artists who specialized in working in those materials. Behan, describing his pleasure at winning the commission to design his Co. Mayo and New York monuments, admitted that he had never really considered the Famine as a theme in his work until then *(Ireland's Great Hunger, An Gorta Mór).*

Figure 8 | John Behan, *National Famine Memorial*

Bronze is expensive. Its choice for artworks on the scale of Behan's two ships, speaks of an Ireland that could now, finally, afford (not just financially, but also psychologically) to look at the absence of commemorative memorials in the country. Indeed, the sudden proliferation of bronze monuments to the Famine toward the end of the 1990s could almost be described as sculptural "bling," were it not for the tragic past to which they refer. Ireland and Irish emigrants around the globe, coming from a more secure and prosperous world, could finally come to own the well of loss at the center of their history. If, as Fionna Barber has pointed out, "In the 1840s the Irish peasantry were the very example of, in Marx's terms, a class unable to represent themselves," by the 1990s, a new class of Celtic Tiger business people and politicians thought they could do it on their behalf. In this instance the memorials function less as means to remember and grieve and more as vehicles of self-congratulation for what we have achieved. A bronze plaque naming those wealthy donors who gave to Norma Smurfit's project serves to underline the new corporate ownership of that past. It distracts attention from Gillespie's work and from the subject it commemorates.

the Famine story has come to be dominated by the theme of survival, of triumph over appalling tragedy

The locations of these sculptural monuments are as significant as the works themselves. Behan's *National Famine Memorial* (1997) is sited on the west coast of Ireland, as the government planned. Its form and location were intended to refer both to the great numbers of deaths from hunger and disease in Ireland, on board the "coffin" ships bound for America and other places and also to the disease of emigration itself. However, the actual placing of this particular memorial, close to what is both a busy tourist route and a sacred site at the foot of Croagh Patrick mountain, turns it into a spectacle, evoking some of the commercial impulses that helped to shape the official response to Paul Henry's landscapes. Its partner, *Arrival* (2000), shows the living embarking on American soil. *Arrival* was commissioned as a gift from Ireland to the United Nations and is displayed in a prominent and cosmopolitan location outside the United Nations Headquarters in New York. It asserts the right of a very different Ireland to display its victory over adversity and its right to a place in the corridors of power. For Irish America, the Famine story has come to be dominated by the theme of survival, of triumph over appalling tragedy. This is the message of Robert Shure's *Boston Irish Famine Memorial* (1998), repeated in the *Philadelphia Irish Memorial* (2003), by Glenna Goodacre and in *The Arrival* (2007) in Toronto, by Rowan Gillespie. Famine at home becomes the birth myth abroad.

Figure 9 | John Behan, *Arrival*

Such interpretations of the Famine narrative bear out the analyses of Lyotard and Rogoff, that the presence of the monument is less about commemorating the event it is named for than it is a marker for a new phase in that history. Rogoff believes that the supposition that the symbolic object (the monument) can replace absence and that memory can be recovered directly or indirectly is wrong. We are still left with the task of living and working with absence (103). Rogoff goes on to suggest that we should stop thinking of absence as a lack that can be filled by the creation of the monument, or as a way of closing off the emotions that the event still arouses and, with them, the event itself. Instead we should keep ourselves open to similar contemporary situations. Referring to Daniel Liebeskind's Holocaust Memorial Museum in Berlin, she argues; "By insisting the events commemorated are part of the historic past, the museum cuts them off from contemporary parallels and limits the range of our understanding of just how complex and far reaching those [historic] continuities could possibly be" (107). Elsewhere in the same paper she says "No inclusion can take place without a loss at the heart of the inclusive art project" (103) The birth myths of Irish-America displace the memories of the Famine, just as Celtic Tiger prosperity in Ireland (albeit short-lived) risked reworking the Famine, less as a disaster on an unspeakable scale, than as a yardstick to measure current success. Rowan Gillespie's *Famine* (1997) group, plodding hopelessly toward the quayside to emigrate, do so against the architecture of Ireland's Financial Services Centre, positing a forlorn past alongside what appeared to be a gleaming future. Spread out along the footpath, they jostle for a place amidst the surging new world of business and high finance leaving no room for contemplating the harsh realities that global capitalism has impinged on small developing economies past and present.

birth myths of Irish-America displace
the memories of the Famine, just as
Celtic Tiger prosperity in Ireland (albeit
short-lived) risked reworking the Famine

Not all monuments to the Famine diaspora follow this route, however. The seemingly endless lists (in reality just over half of the 1,124 who died, at Éireann Quay, Toronto, in 1847) of emigrants' names carved into Kilkenny limestone in Ireland Park, Toronto (2007), and the sheets of glass etched to the design of Angela and Hossein Valamanesh with the names of Irish orphan girls at the *Australian Monument to the Great Irish Famine* (1999) at Hyde Park Barracks, Sydney, do not attempt to superimpose a narrative on the actual event. They simply provide a place to remember and mourn. By resisting the traditional response of specific figurative presences, and by opting instead for a symbolic language—text, and specifically lists of names—they link Ireland's mass tragedy to a new postmodern alternative form for the grand-narrative, initiated by Maya Lin's *Vietnam Veterans Memorial* (1982) wall in Washington, D.C., which combines the collective with the singular. Instead of the narrative monument that turns the horror of war into glorious achievement, the wall reveals the enormity of the loss as name is added to name. Likewise, the limestone slabs bearing the names of the 19th-century Irish who died en route to Toronto, become a cliff face, carried all the way from Ireland in the wake of those they commemorate. In Sydney, the etched names of the orphan girls, sent out from Ireland to work for an uncertain future in Australia, cast shadows through the glass on to the wall behind, suggesting the layers of history that conceal their stories. In place of the grand narrative, these name-bearing walls become monuments to the nameless, the non-heroes, those who were actually there.

Figure 10 | Brian Tolle. *Irish Hunger Memorial*

The *Irish Hunger Memorial* in Battery Park City, New York [Figure 10], was partly built from the excavation of the World Trade Center's foundations and is dedicated to both the Irish Famine and world hunger. Brian Tolle avoided depictions of Famine victims too. Instead, he created a sloping field using earth, fossils and plants from Ireland, as well as rocks salvaged from the 1970s construction site and topped this with a derelict Famine cottage. The result is a rocky, quarter-acre plot, exactly the size of holding that disqualified the owners and their families from Poor Law relief in Ireland in 1847. The work represents the absent original occupants through nearly two miles of text, from letters, snatches of biographies, folklore, poems, songs and recipes, presented in bands on the tunnel-like entrance from the street below. Those quotations are blended with references to contemporary famines and issues around consumption and obesity in Western society. Chosen in collaboration with Maureen Murphy, author of the New York State curriculum on world hunger, these texts are presented ahistorically, avoiding chronology and in a strictly democratic manner. The entrance passageway, with its stone lintel, refers the visitor back to the megalithic passage graves scattered around Ireland, while all around the memorial, one of the world's most energetic centers of capitalism pursues its daily business. For Tolle, that juxtaposition was a reminder of what is essential. He is insistent that "hunger is not abstract. It is a fundamental problem of human condition" ("Interview" 4).

Attempts to re-create a sense of the actual event in the visual idiom of the 19th century stress the difference between then and now. Perhaps that is why they are so appealing to those who want to say that history is over. The model for commemorative sculpture inherited by the Irish in the 20th century derives from the monuments to British imperial achievement that proliferated all over the country. To try to fit Ireland's very different history to that model is as impossible as it is inappropriate, giving us public memorials that reflect what James Joyce called the "cracked looking glass of a servant"[7] in place of a vibrant, creative and inclusive collective model. By not adhering to that model and by not imposing human figures to represent us in their Famine artworks, Alanna O'Kelly and Brian Tolle turn us from spectators into personal participants. We walk Tolle's quarter acre, wondering how we could support a family from it, look at the "big houses" of capitalism all around us and wonder what they have in store for us next. Or we become the owner of the disembodied panting for breath on a road that might lead to Doolough or Darfur in O'Kelly's 1996 work *A Beathú*. History is not over. We are still living within it, not outside it. That is why there is provision to review and update the quotations in Tolle's memorial every year.

feelings of shame for having survived, allied to intense awareness that such trauma could be visited upon others in the future, is enough to bring about the silence

For Tolle, a further consideration in making a public memorial was the history of presentation itself. He was very conscious of the difference between showing an artwork in a museum where the wider history becomes subjected to the authority of the institution and how artwork is mediated by its position in a public space. The two museums dedicated to the Great Hunger, the Famine Museum in Strokestown, Co. Roscommon, and Ireland's Great Hunger Museum at Quinnipiac University are themselves monuments, but monuments of a very different kind. The Strokestown museum takes its *raison d'etre* from the Strokestown Estate Papers and archaeological evidence of the Famine and the "big house" and tenant relations in its aftermath. Ireland's Great Hunger Museum works in a different way, gathering together original documents, such as the British Parliamentary Papers, newspapers and news illustrations, and original letters as well as artworks by artists on both sides of the Atlantic, from the figurative sculpture of Glenna Goodacre and Rowan Gillespie to paintings by Hughie O'Donoghue, Brian Maguire and Micheal Farrell. The museum commissioned Margaret Lyster Chamberlain to make *The Leave-Taking* (2000) **[Figure 11]**, a work with 16 bronze figures that is inspired as much by the Holocaust as by the Irish Famine. Chamberlain explains her process saying: "I went within myself to integrate this experience into each figure's persona" (*IGHM* 46). The figurative element in *Statistic I* **[Figure 12]**, perhaps Gillespie's most successful artwork about the

Figure 11 | Margaret Lyster Chamberlain, *The Leave-Taking*

Figure 12 | Rowan Gillespie, *Statistic I*

Famine, now in the collection of Ireland's Great Hunger Museum, is based directly on the well-known image of "Bridget O'Donnel and her children" from *The Illustrated London News*, while the lists of names set into the simple, bronze base she stands on remind us of those who died and the Famine-related diseases that caused their deaths. Brian Maguire's work has always been driven by consciousness of contemporary suffering. This is the correlative for the historic experience in Maguire's painting, *The World is Full of Murder* (1985, IGHM). Hughie O'Donoghue, brought up within an Irish immigrant family in Manchester, was deeply affected by the emotions his visits to his mother's family home in County Mayo aroused, and the collective and personal memories associated with the place and its history. Through his use of color, scale and surface effects, he creates an abstract tension and energy that involves the viewer very powerfully [Figure 13]. Living in France and influenced by the intellectualism of French discourse on history, particularly its republican tradition, Micheal Farrell, in *Black '47* (1997–98, IGHM), exposes the human actions that turn natural failure into outright disaster.

What do these responses to a far-reaching event in Irish history tell us? To begin with, they show that certain events are too traumatic to be turned into singular, closed, heroic monuments. While survival of the horrors discussed here is itself heroic, the complexity of the emotional burden left in their wake cannot be easily communicated and discharged. The feelings of shame for having survived, allied to intense awareness that such trauma could be visited upon others in the future, is enough to bring about the silence that was the most significant response in Ireland from several generations. Poverty is shaming and alienating, although that shame is more often carried unfairly by its victims than by those who cause it. The kind of abject poverty that saw one million people die of starvation and forced many more to give their children up to the care of strangers is utterly demeaning. The theory of ambiguous loss outlined by the psychologist Pauline Boss offers useful insights into the need for finality for those who have suffered loss of loved ones from major catastrophe, e.g., where they have not been able to find and bury their dead. In Ireland this is understood and reflected in a simple but devastating question carved into the boulder that forms the base of a Famine memorial in Doolough Valley in County Mayo that bears the following text: "How can men feel themselves honoured by the humiliation of their fellow beings?" The words belong to Mahatma Gandhi, but many Irish people must have asked the same question.

abject poverty that saw one million
people die of starvation and forced many
more to give their children up to the care
of strangers is utterly demeaning

The question, then, is not whether the Irish people suffer from amnesia but how, now that we are finally able to examine this history, can we commemorate it in a manner that is empowering and liberating rather than a perpetual plea for sympathy in the face of changing national and international contexts? As Adorno so movingly explained about Jewish experience, "After Auschwitz our feelings... baulk at squeezing any kind of sense, however bleached, out of the victim's fate" (361). Both he and Sarah Kofman insist that the Holocaust must never happen again. That means that Kofman and Adorno believe that they "can only memorialise the Shoah in a way that is without 'result' or profit for speculative thought" (Dobie xix). Can it be said that Irish memorials to the Great Hunger are inspired by such lofty ideals, not tainted by thought of political or commercial gain, but driven instead by the need to make sure that famine is eliminated for all time? While art should never be a vehicle for propaganda, it can and does position itself politically in the world, and it is the official political dimension that is all too often highlighted in public commemorative projects. Paul Ricoeur calls for what he terms an ethical approach to memory, for amnesty rather than amnesia in relation to the wounds of history. He recommends that instead of allowing ourselves to be repetitively locked into a sense of the past that leads to resentment, we should open ourselves up to the invention of history, that is an approach to history that is at once imaginative, interpretative and creative, and at the same time, we should be aware of history as an inventory. If we know about our history we just might be able to learn from it.

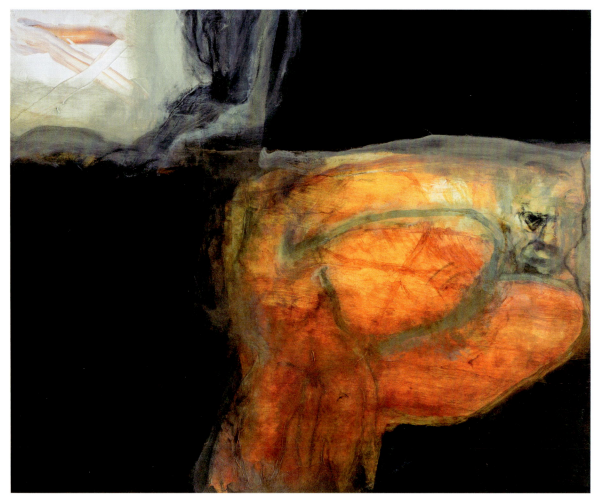

Figure 13 | Hughie O'Donoghue, *On Our Knees*

It is impossible to recreate the past, however much some historians or politicians might wish, because we ourselves are shaped by the present. The sensibility we bring to bear on the past separates us from it and condemns attempts to recreate it, through some kind of mimesis, to failure. If artists do not use the most challenging contemporary forms of expression to interpret the past, they are denying their own place in the dialogue between past and present. Artists like Brian Tolle, Alanna O'Kelly, Brian Maguire and Hughie O'Donoghue, do not seek to recreate the past.

If artists do not use the most challenging contemporary forms of expression to interpret the past, they are denying their own place in the dialogue

Instead, by acknowledging their own position in the present, as people with an eye to the future, as well as an informed view of the past, they create the kind of disorientated, imaginative space that allows us to enter aspects of it, which has the potential to help us to work through past pain, to declare an amnesty toward it and to strengthen us for the future. Asenath Nicholson described the workhouses as the real monuments to the Famine. To these we could add the work of those who were there—the "relief" projects, many of them futile, which still survive all over the country. Perhaps with the help of the artists we can begin to do that.

ENDNOTES

[1] Words by Mahatma Gandhi, carved on the Famine Memorial (1997), Doolough Valley, Co. Mayo. Taken from Gandhi's autobiography, *The Story of My Experiments with Truth*. 2 vols. 1927–29.

[2] Margaret Kelleher (2002). She refers to, among others, historians Roy Foster and Niall O'Ciosáin and cultural theorist David Lloyd.

[3] Discussed also in Kelleher (2002) and Patsy McGarry, "Roots of a warped view of sexuality." *The Irish Times*, Weekend Review. June 20, 2009.

[4] See also Katie Donovan, "How should we commemorate the Famine?" *The Irish Times*, October 12, 1994.

[5] See Margaret Kelleher (2002) for a useful summary.

[6] The Irish War of Independence against Britain that had begun with the failed Easter Rising in 1916, broke out again in 1919 and continued as a guerrilla war until December 1921. During that period and in its aftermath, British holidaymakers felt unsafe in Ireland and tended to avoid the country.

[7] See James Joyce, *Ulysses* (1922). Chapter 1. "Telemachus." Section 1, line 131.

WORKS CITED

Adorno, T. W. *Negative Dialectics*. Trans. E. B. Ashton, 1973. New York: Seabury Press, 1979. Print.

Arnold, Bruce. "Monument to one Artist's True Genius." October 13, 2009. <http://www.brucearnold. ie/pages/art_files/momuments-genius.php >.

Barber, Fionna. "Alanna O'Kelly's *Sanctuary/Wasteland*: Location, Memory and Hunger in Recent Irish Visual Culture." Social History Society Annual Conference, University of Rouen. January 9, 2004. Address.

Benson, Ciaran. *The Cultural Psychology of Self: Place Morality and Art in Human Worlds*. London: Routledge, 2001. Print.

Boss, Pauline. "Ambiguous Loss Research, Theory, and Practice: Reflections After 9/11." *Journal of Marriage and Family*. Vol. 66. No. 3 (August 2004): 551–66. Print. Web. March 25, 2014. < DOI: 10.1111/ j.0022-2445.2004.00037 >.

Brown, Terence. "Foreword." *The Hungry Voice: The Poetry of the Irish Famine*. Ed. Chris Morash. Dublin and Portland, OR: Irish Academic Press, 1989. Print.

Daly, Mary. "1916 as the national commemoration? The paradox." "Object Matters: Making 1916. A conference on the material and visual culture of the Easter Rising." Dublin City Council Civic Offices, Wood Quay. April 26, 2013. Keynote address.

Davis, Thomas. *The Nation*. October 15, 1842.

Dobie, Madeline. Translator's Introduction. *Smothered Words*. Sarah Kofman. Evanston, IL: Northwestern University Press, 1998. Print.

Freeman's Journal. Dublin. April 6, 1843.

Ireland's Great Hunger: An Gorta Mór: The Quinnipiac University Collection. Dir. Turlough McConnell, n.d. DVD.

Ireland's Great Hunger Museum Inaugural Catalogue. Hamden, CT: Quinnipiac University, 2012. Print.

Kelleher, Margaret. *The Feminization of Famine*. Durham: Duke University Press, 1997. Print.

---. "Hunger and History: Monuments to the Great Irish Famine," *Textual Practice* 16. 2 (2002) 249–76. Print. Web. March 25, 2014. < DOI: 10.1080/095023602761622342 >.

Lloyd, David. "The Memory of Hunger." *Loss: The Politics of Mourning*. Eds. David L. Eng and David Kazanjian. Berkeley: University of California Press, 2003. Print.

Lyotard, Jean-François. *The Postmodern Condition: A Report on Knowledge*. 1979. Minneapolis: University of Minnesota Press, 1984. Print.

McGarry, Patsy. "Roots of a warped view of sexuality," *The Irish Times*, June 20, 2009.

O'Donoghue, Hughie. *Naming the Fields*. Dublin: Rubicon Gallery, 2001. Print.

Póirtéir, Cathal. "The Folklore of the Famine: Seanchas an Drochshaoil." *Atlas of the Great Irish Famine*. Eds. Crowley, Smyth and Murphy. Cork: Cork University Press, 2012. Print.

Ricoeur, Paul, *Memory, History, Forgetting*. Trans. Kathleen Blamey and David Pellauer. Chicago: Univeristy of Chicago Press, 2004. Print.

Rogoff, Irit. "Reading the Agreement." *The Civil Arts Enquiry: Documents*. City Arts Center, Dublin, 2003.

Tolle, Brian. "Interview with Brian Tolle, by Carlos Motta." *artwurl.org, INT018* <http://www.carlosmotta. com/writings/BrianTolle.pdf>. n.d. Web. March 25, 2014.

Turpin, John. "Oliver Sheppard's 1798 Memorials." *Irish Arts Review Yearbook* (1990-1991): 71.

Usherwood, Paul, and Jenny Spencer-Smith. *Lady Butler, Battle Artist, 1846–1933*. Gloucester: Alan Sutton, 1987. Print.

Walker, J. Crampton. *Irish Life and Landscape*. Dublin: Talbot Press, 1926. n.p.

Waters, John. "Confronting the ghosts of our past." *Irish hunger: Personal Reflections on the Legacy of the Famine*. Ed. Tom Hayden. Colorado: Roberts Rinehart, 1979. 29. Print.

IMAGES

Cover

Alanna O'Kelly
b. 1955

A Kind of Quietism [detail]
1990
Photo text
3 panels 19.7 x 29.5 in
3 panels 19.7 x 14.6 in
© 1990 Alanna O'Kelly

Figure 1

Brian Tolle
b. 1964

Irish Hunger Memorial
2001-2002
Various materials
one-half acre site
Battery Park, New York
Image provided by
Brian Tolle Studio

Figure 2

Glenna Goodacre
b. 1939

Anguish
Bronze on wood base
17 x 12.5 x 13 in
© Glenna Goodacre

Figure 3

Erskine Nicol, ARA
1825-1904

A Knotty Point
1853
Oil on mill board
11 x 14.25 in

Figure 4

Lilian Lucy Davidson
1879-1954

Gorta
1946
Oil on canvas
27.5 x 35.5 in
© Estate of Lilian Lucy Davidson

Figure 5

Paul Henry, RHA
1876-1958

Cottages, West of Ireland
1928-30
Oil on canvas
22 x 26 in
© Estate of Paul Henry,
IVARO, Dublin 2014

Figure 6

Edward Delaney
1930-2009

Famine Memorial
1967
Bronze
Saint Stephen's Green, Dublin
Photo by William Morrison, 2011

Figure 7

Alanna O'Kelly
b. 1955

*No Colouring Can Deepen
the Darkness of Truth*
1994-2012
Compilation of still images
from video installation
© 1992, Alanna O'Kelly

Figure 8

John Behan, RHA
b. 1938

National Famine Memorial
1997
Bronze
26 x 20 ft
Murrisk, Co. Mayo.
© John Behan

Figure 9

John Behan, RHA
b. 1938

Arrival
2001
Cast Bronze
22 ft 11.5 in x 26 ft 8.5 in
United Nations Plaza, New York
© John Behan

Figure 10

Brian Tolle
b. 1964

Irish Hunger Memorial
2001-2002
Various materials
one-half acre site
Battery Park, New York
Photo by Stan Ries
Image provided by
Brian Tolle Studio

Figure 11

Margaret Lyster Chamberlain
b. 1954

The Leave-Taking
2000
Cast bronze
25 x 36 x 12 in
© 2000 Margaret Lyster Chamberlain

Figure 12

Rowan Gillespie
b. 1953

Statistic I
2010
Bronze
49 x 19 x 19 in
© 2010, Rowan Gillespie

Figure 13

Hughie O'Donoghue
b. 1953

On Our Knees
1996-1997
Acrylic
48 x 60 in
© 1996-97 Hughie O'Donoghue

Images provided by
Ireland's Great Hunger Museum,
Quinnipiac University,
unless noted otherwise.